The Science of Living Things

What is a Plant?

Bobbie Kalman

 Crabtree Publishing Company

The Science of Living Things Series
A Bobbie Kalman Book

**To Kelly Glozier
for her beauty and resilience**

Author and Editor-in-Chief
Bobbie Kalman

Managing Editor
Lynda Hale

Reasearch and Project Editors
Niki Walker
Kate Calder

Copy Editors
Heather Fitzpatrick
Hannelore Sotzek
John Crossingham

Computer Design
Lynda Hale

Production Coordinator
Hannelore Sotzek

Photo Researcher
Kate Calder

Consultant
Ronald Dengler,
Professor of Botany, University of Toronto

Photographs
Lynda Hale: page 17
Bobbie Kalman: page 13
Robert McCaw: page 21 (top)
Photo Researchers, Inc./Kjell B. Sandved: pages 12-13;
    Merlin D. Tuttle, Bat Conservation International: page 20
Tom Stack & Associates: Ken W. Davis: page 16;
    John Shaw: page 21 (bottom) ; Robert Winslow: page 5 (top)
Other images by Digital Stock and Eyewire, Inc.

Illustrations
Barbara Bedell: pages 4, 11 (bottom both), 13 (top), 14,
    18, 19 (bottom), 22 (all except daffodil), 23, 24, 25
Bonna Rouse: pages 6-7, 9, 10, 11 (top three), 13 (bottom),
    15, 16, 17, 19 (top), 22 (daffodil), 30-31

Digital Prepress
Embassy Graphics

Printer
Worzalla Publishing Company

Crabtree Publishing Company

PMB 16A	612 Welland Ave.	73 Lime Walk
350 Fifth Ave.,	St. Catharines	Headington,
Suite 3308	Ontario,	Oxford
New York, NY	Canada	OX3 7AD
10118	L2M 5V6	United Kingdom

Cataloging in Publication Data
Kalman, Bobbie
    What is a plant?

(The science of living things)
Includes index.

ISBN 0-86505-982-9 (library bound) ISBN 0-86505-959-4 (pbk.)
This book introduces plant life, discussing specific types such as
carnivorous and parasitic plants, and concepts such as single cells,
germination, and photosynthesis.

1. Plants—Juvenile literature. 2. Botany—Juvenile literature. [1. Plants.
2. Botany.] I. Title. II. Series: Kalman, Bobbie. Science of living things.

QK49.K16 2000   j580   LC 99-085749
                                                            CIP

Contents

Living things need plants

Most living things on Earth depend on plants. Plants provide people and animals with food and shelter. They also produce much of the **oxygen** in the air. Oxygen is a gas that people and animals need to breathe.

Plants grow wherever there is enough sunshine and water for making food. They use sunlight and water to produce food inside their leaves or stem. Plants make their own food, but they are also a source of food for other living things.

Many animals get energy from eating the plants in this grassy field. The energy from the plants is then passed on to other animals, which eat the animals that have eaten the plants.

Homes for animals

Plant life is home to animals and insects of every shape and size. Squirrels and monkeys make their homes in trees. Birds use plant materials such as twigs, grass, and leaves to build nests.

Air fresheners

When plants make food, they take in **carbon dioxide**, a gas in the air that is poisonous to people and animals. They produce oxygen, which makes the air fresher to breathe.

The world's air conditioners

Carbon dioxide traps the sun's heat and causes Earth's temperature to rise above normal. This heating is called the **greenhouse effect**.

Without plants, Earth would become hotter and hotter. By taking carbon dioxide from the air, plants help keep the Earth at a stable temperature. Plants also release water into the air, which lowers the temperature.

(right) In areas with many trees, such as in rain forests, the air is fresh and moist.

(above) Foxes often make their den in fallen logs. Red fox cubs leave their den in the spring.

What are plants?

Plants are living things that come in thousands of shapes and sizes. Some are small enough to hold on the tip of your finger, and others are the tallest, heaviest living things on Earth. Even though they look different, all plants have three important things in common:

1. They are made up of more than one **cell**.
2. They are able to make their own food.
3. They are green.

Water plants are found in ponds, rivers, lakes, and oceans. Their roots, stems, and leaves are suited to living partially or completely underwater. They provide food and shelter for wetland animals and fish.

The green kingdom

All plants belong to the plant **kingdom**. A kingdom is a group of living things that shares similar characteristics. There are more than 300,000 different **species**, or types, of plants. Look at the examples of plants on these two pages.

Seed plants

Many plants grow from seeds. A plant needs the pollen from another plant to produce seeds. (See page 18.)

Flowering plants are the largest group of plants, with more than 250,000 known species.

*Some plants eat meat! The pitcher plant, shown right, is a **carnivorous** plant. It traps and eats insects and spiders.*

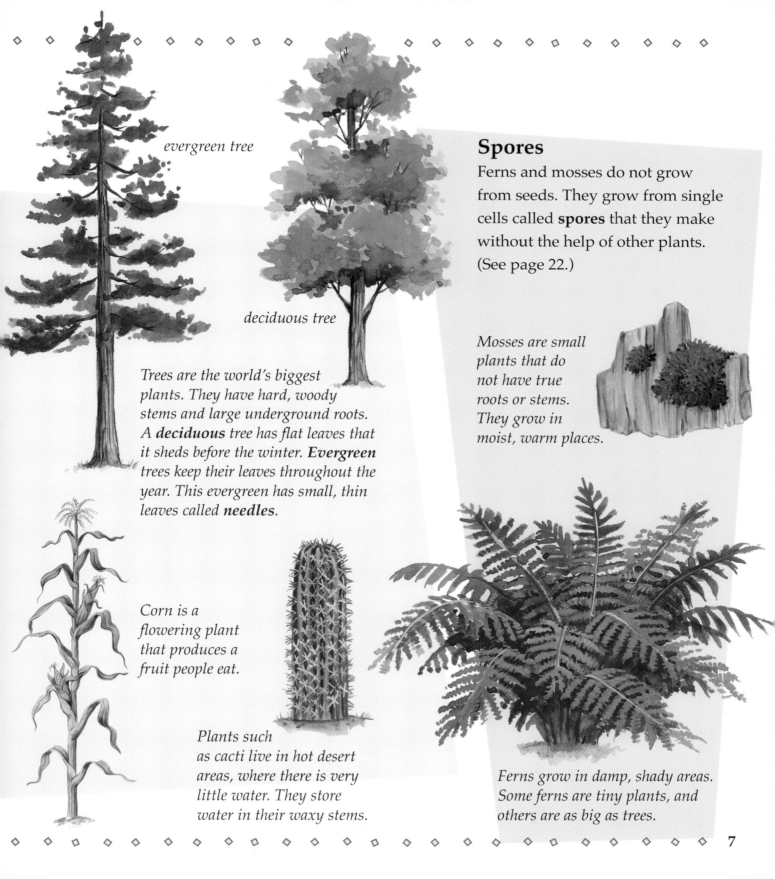

evergreen tree

deciduous tree

Spores

Ferns and mosses do not grow from seeds. They grow from single cells called **spores** that they make without the help of other plants. (See page 22.)

Mosses are small plants that do not have true roots or stems. They grow in moist, warm places.

*Trees are the world's biggest plants. They have hard, woody stems and large underground roots. A **deciduous** tree has flat leaves that it sheds before the winter. **Evergreen** trees keep their leaves throughout the year. This evergreen has small, thin leaves called **needles**.*

Corn is a flowering plant that produces a fruit people eat.

Plants such as cacti live in hot desert areas, where there is very little water. They store water in their waxy stems.

Ferns grow in damp, shady areas. Some ferns are tiny plants, and others are as big as trees.

not a plant

Many living things look or behave like plants, but scientists do not include them in the plant kingdom. Corals, mushrooms, **lichens**, **algae**, and seaweeds are not plants. Corals and sea fans belong to the animal kingdom.

Mushrooms are **fungi**. Algae and seaweeds belong to yet another kingdom. They are **protists**, or living things that have simple cell structures. Lichens are organisms that are created when algae grows on a fungus.

Mushrooms and other fungi may look like plants, but they cannot make their own food as plants can.

This piece of wood has green, slimy algae growing on it. Algae are not plants, but they can make their own food. They help keep millions of ocean animals alive.

sea fan

Lichen is made up of an alga and a fungus that have a **symbiotic** relationship. Each relies on the other for its survival. The fungus takes in water and nutrients. The alga uses these materials to make food for itself and the fungus.

coral

Sometimes appearances can fool you! Corals, sponges, and sea fans may look like plants, but they actually are animals.

Seaweeds

Seaweeds are a type of alga. Most scientists do not consider seaweeds to be plants, but they are similar to the first plants that grew on Earth. Just like the plants of long ago, seaweeds also have no true roots, stems, or leaves. Seaweeds come in all sizes from tiny to 200 feet (61 m) long. Seaweed is used for food or as fertilizer.

Roots, stems, and leaves

Plants differ in shape and size, but most have roots, leaves, and a stem. Each part has its own job to do to help the plant survive. Look at the pictures on these pages to find out how these parts work together.

bud

pedicel →
(flower stalk)

petiole →
(leaf stalk)

Leaves absorb sunlight and make food for the plant. They can be large or small, flat or needle-like. Large leaves absorb a lot of sunlight. Small, thin leaves keep in moisture. Leaves are suited to help plants survive in their environment.

Most stems hold the plant upright.

blade of leaf

The vascular system

A network of tubes called the **vascular system** connects all the parts of a plant. One set of tubes, called **xylem**, carries water and nutrients from the roots to the stem, leaves, and flowers. Another set, called **phloem**, carries food from the leaves to the rest of the plant. The soft tissue in the center of the plant is the **pith**. Pith cells store extra food.

xylem

pith

phloem

Roots anchor the plant in the soil and take in water and nutrients, which the plant uses to make food. A tough **root cap** protects the root tip as it grows and pushes through the soil.

At the root

There are three basic types of roots—**taproots**, **fibrous** roots, and **adventitious** roots.

Adventitious roots develop from the stem. They enable plants such as ivy to climb up walls.

Fibrous roots are thin roots that branch out in all directions near the surface of the ground. Many desert plants have fibrous roots to help them trap as much water as possible from the morning dew.

A taproot is a main root that has many smaller roots growing from it. The taproot becomes much larger and thicker as it grows.

*The **epidermis**, or skin, of most leaves is covered by a waxy coating called the **cuticle**. The cuticle protects the leaf and keeps it moist.*

(left) This plant stalk has two leaves that each have three leaflets.

Leaves

You can identify a plant by the structure of its leaves. A leaf can have one leaf blade or several leaf blades, or **leaflets**.

(right) Compound leaves are divided into several leaflets. This plant has three compound leaves.

11

Staying alive

Plants are found all over the world in deserts, forests, bodies of water, on mountaintops, and in the freezing Arctic. To survive in harsh environments, plants have **adapted**, or changed slowly, to suit their surroundings. They have many ways of staying alive and protecting themselves.

Water plants

Water plants have pockets of air in their stem and leaves that help them float. Many absorb nutrients from the water through their leaves. Some have very long roots.

Desert plants

Desert plants do not waste a single drop of water. Some have huge fibrous roots that soak up dew or rainfall. Others have long roots that can reach water deep underground. Desert plants have a waxy coating that keeps moisture from escaping. They store water in their thick stem. Having no leaves prevents cacti from losing moisture. Their sharp spines help keep animals from eating them.

Tropical plants

The thick vegetation in a tropical forest does not allow much light to reach the forest floor. Many plants have wide leaves to catch as much sunlight as possible. Some plants such as vines, shown below, grow up trees to reach sunlight.

(left) Arctic poppies have tiny hairs on their stems that help keep in warmth and moisture.

(below) Mosses grow on rocks, which shelter them from the wind.

Surviving the cold

Plants that live in the Arctic and high on mountaintops face strong winds, freezing temperatures, and little rainfall. They grow low to the ground to avoid wind, which can batter their leaves and dry them out. They have small leaves that lose little water. Many are covered in fine hairs that act as a blanket to help hold in heat.

Defending themselves

Plants are easy targets for hungry animals and insects, but they have developed many ways of protecting themselves. Some plants have poison in their leaves, fruits, or seeds that can make an animal sick or even kill it. Others have hollow, brittle hairs that are filled with poison. When an animal brushes against the plant, the hairs scratch its skin and the poison causes a painful itch or sting. Other plants disguise themselves to avoid enemies. Stone plants, shown left, are able to hide because they look just like small pebbles. This type of disguise is called **mimicry**.

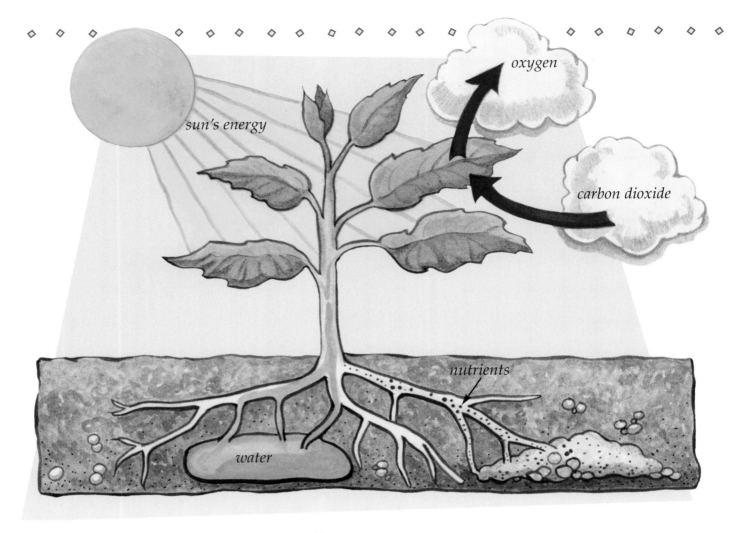

The plant takes in sunlight, carbon dioxide, water, and nutrients to make food. In the process of making food, it releases oxygen into the air.

Making Food

Plants use the energy from the sun to make food. This process is called **photosynthesis**. Photosynthesis only happens when there is sunlight. A plant's leaves contain a green substance called **chlorophyll**. Chlorophyll absorbs energy from the sun. The plant uses the sun's energy to change carbon dioxide and water into food. The food that the plant creates is **glucose**, a type of sugar. Glucose travels throughout the plant in a liquid called **sap**.

Moving toward light

Plants cannot travel from place to place the way animals can, but they are able to move their stems, roots, and leaves to get the sunlight and water they need for photosynthesis. Plants sense where there is water, and their roots grow toward it. The stems and leaves of plants grow toward the sun or light such as a lamp.

Sunflowers turn to face the sun. As the sun moves across the sky throughout the day, the sunflower's top keeps turning to face it.

A leaf cell

Cells are the smallest living things. They can be seen only through a microscope. All living things are made up of cells. Some are single-celled, and others are made of millions of cells. A cell has a **membrane**, or outer wall, that holds it together. The **nucleus** controls what the cell does. Each type of cell has a different job. The plant cell shown here is found in a leaf. It has **chloroplasts**, which help the plant make its food. Its **vacuole** stores food and gets larger as the plant takes in water.

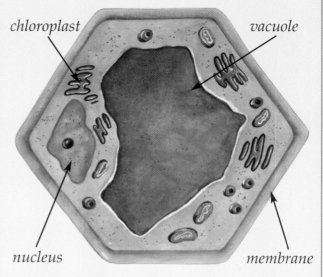

chloroplast *vacuole*

nucleus *membrane*

Other ways of getting food

This insect has landed on a sundew and is now stuck. The sundew uses its sticky juices to eat the insect.

Even though plants make their own food, some also feed on insects, spiders, and small animals such as mice and frogs. These meat-eaters are called carnivorous plants. They use their leaves to trap and kill their **prey**, or the animals they eat. Most carnivorous plants live in ponds or marshes where there are not enough nutrients. They need to feed on meat to get the extra nutrients they need.

Venus flytrap

The Venus flytrap is an **active trapper**. It catches prey that touch the **trigger hairs** on its leaf. When the plant catches its prey, digestive juices ooze from the leaf. They break down the prey's soft parts so the plant can use them, but they cannot break down hard parts such as wings or bones.

trigger hairs

The leaf of the Venus flytrap is hinged in the middle and has three trigger hairs on each half. When an insect lands on a leaf and moves two of the three trigger hairs, the leaf snaps shut around it. The halves lock together to hold the insect or, sometimes, a frog inside.

mistletoe

apple tree

Feeding off other plants

Parasitic plants survive by getting their food from other plants. These plants attach themselves to a **host** plant and steal its food and nutrients. A host plant often dies when a parasitic plant attaches itself to it. Most parasitic plants have small leaves that contain little chlorophyll. Without enough chlorophyll, plants are unable to make their own food. The mistletoe is partially parasitic—it grows its roots directly into an apple tree to get nutrients, but it also has leaves for making its own food.

The strangler fig tree

The strangler fig tree uses another tree for support. From a high branch of the host tree, the strangler fig grows roots. The roots grow to reach the ground and surround the host tree. The host tree rots away. The strangler fig tree shown below caused the host tree's trunk to fall onto a nearby tree. The long roots formed a curtain that reaches the ground.

The new fig tree begins to grow high in a host tree.

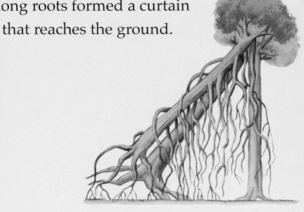

The fig tree and host tree fall onto a nearby tree.

The roots grow to the ground, creating a curtain.

Growing from seeds

stigma

stamen

ovaries

Although flowers are different in color, shape, and size, they all have the same parts. Their stamens and stigma are used in pollination, and their ovaries turn into fruit that contain seeds.

Flowers are beautiful to look at, but they have a much more important job than pleasing people. Flowers are designed for **pollination**, which is the first step in making seeds. Pollination takes place when pollen from one flower's **stamen** reaches another flower's **stigma**. After a flower is pollinated, its petals fall off. The ovaries inside the flower grow larger and become fruit. The fruit contains the seeds for the next plant.

Taking root

A seed is a capsule that contains a tiny **embryo**, or new plant. It also contains a supply of food for the embryo to use as it grows. All embryos have a **radicle**, which grows into the soil and becomes a root. When a seed lands in a spot with enough space and water, it begins to **germinate**, or grow into a new plant. When the new plant starts growing leaves, it can begin using water and sunlight to make its own food.

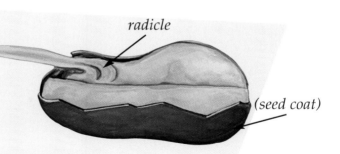

radicle

(seed coat)

The seed absorbs water until its coat cracks, and the radicle pushes through the soil. Soon after, the first shoot pushes its way up through the soil.

A flowering plant's life cycle

These pictures show four stages in the life cycle of a flowering plant. The pod of this bean plant is its fruit, and the beans are its seeds.

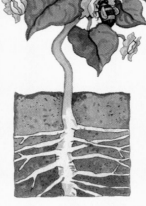

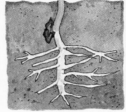

1. The seed breaks open. The radicle grows downward, and a stem grows up.

2. The young bean plant grows leaves and starts making its own food.

3. Insects bring pollen from other bean plants to pollinate the flowers of this plant.

4. A fruit forms around the seeds. The fruit and seed fall to the ground.

Help from nature

Plants cannot move from place to place, so they need help spreading both their pollen and seeds. Some plants rely on the wind. Others depend on animals such as insects, birds, bats, mice, and slugs to spread their pollen and seeds.

This fruit bat is getting pollen on its face while eating a tasty meal of nectar. Some of this nectar will rub off onto other flowers that the bat will visit.

Mission: attraction

Animals that help spread pollen from plant to plant are called **pollinators**. Many pollinators are attracted to flowers by the bright colors of the petals and the sweet scent that the petals produce. Plants make a liquid called **nectar**, on which the animals feed. The nectar is located in the flower's center, so pollinators get pollen on their body as they try to reach it. An animal then goes to similar flowers to eat nectar and takes the pollen with it. When the pollen reaches the next flower, the pollination process is completed.

Burrs ride on this buffalo's nose to a place where they will fall off and take root.

Seeds on the go

A seed must travel to a new spot so it will not compete with its parent for space and water. When a bird or other animal swallows the seeds in fruit, the seeds are deposited in new places in the droppings of the animals. Some seeds are covered with burrs that stick to an animal's fur. When the hooks on the burrs snap, the seeds fall to the ground. Dandelion seeds ride the breeze using "parachutes." Coconuts float a long way to new land before their seeds grow.

The seeds of milkweed plants are attached to silky white hairs that float in the wind and carry the seed like a parachute.

Other ways of growing

Most plants grow from seeds, but many plants also have another way of **reproducing**. Some grow new plants from their stems. Others produce **bulbs** that store food and grow into new plants. Some plants do not make seeds at all. These plants produce spores that grow into new plants.

Making new ferns

Ferns do not grow from seeds or need pollen from other plants. They make spores on the underside of their **fronds**, or leaves. The spores are released, and some grow into tiny plants called **prothallia**. A new plant sprouts from a prothallium and gets nourishment from it until it can make its own food. The prothallium then dies, and the new plant grows into a leafy fern.

Bulbs

Some plants such as daffodils grow from bulbs that store food. A bulb is a bundle of short, swollen leaves packed tightly around a fat stem. Bulbs grow stems and flowers in warm weather. New bulbs grow on the side of the parent bulb. The bulbs are not active during winter. The new bulbs grow into plants in the spring.

new bulb

new fern

spores

spore cases

Millions of spores grow in tiny spore cases on the bottom of a fern's fronds.

The spore cases break open and release the dustlike spores.

A spore grows into a prothallium, from which a fern grows. The small, curled fern opens as it grows bigger.

Growing from the stem

Some plants grow from stems called **runners**. A small shoot grows from a runner, and the new plant gets nourishment from the parent plant until it grows roots and a stem of its own. It then becomes a separate plant. Some stems grow just under the surface of the ground. These types of stems are called **rhizomes**.

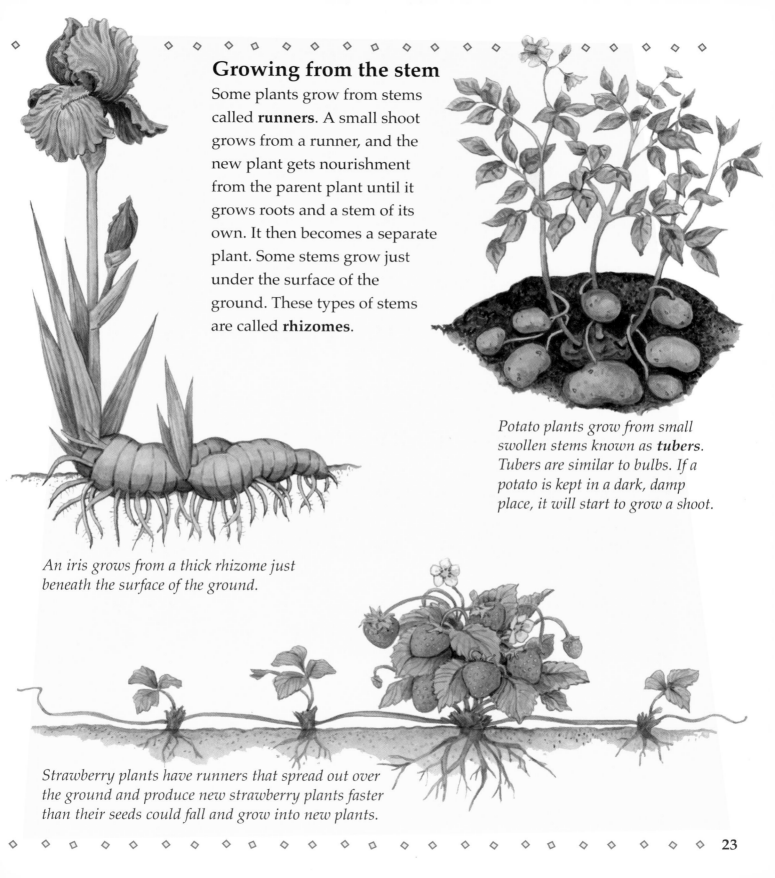

*Potato plants grow from small swollen stems known as **tubers**. Tubers are similar to bulbs. If a potato is kept in a dark, damp place, it will start to grow a shoot.*

An iris grows from a thick rhizome just beneath the surface of the ground.

Strawberry plants have runners that spread out over the ground and produce new strawberry plants faster than their seeds could fall and grow into new plants.

Trees and forests

There are forests all over the world, except in areas near the poles. Cold, northern climates are home to **boreal** forests, which contain evergreen trees. Climates with warm and cold seasons have **mixed** and deciduous forests. Mixed forests have both evergreen and deciduous trees. Tropical **rain forests** are found in climates that are warm all year long.

Conifers produce seeds in cones. Their cones have layers of hard shells that protect the young seeds.

canopy

understory

forest floor

*Tropical rain forests have three layers of plants: the **canopy**, the **understory**, and the **forest floor**.*

Conifers

Evergreens are trees that keep most of their leaves throughout the year. Evergreens that grow in cold climates are called **conifers** because they have cones. Fir, spruce, and pine trees are conifers. They have waxy, needle-like leaves that keep water from evaporating.

Tropical evergreens

Trees grow throughout the entire year in warm tropical climates. They need to be very tall so their leaves will get enough sunlight for photosynthesis. Many grow more than 15 feet (5 m) in one year. Other tropical plants use trees to survive in the rain forest. Vines wrap around tall trees to grow high to reach sunlight. Some plants grow on high tree branches. Their dangling roots take in moisture from the air.

Deciduous trees

Deciduous trees shed their leaves before the winter. In the warm summer months, a tree grows and produces leaves, fruit, and seeds. During the cold, short winter days, there is less sunlight for photosynthesis, and a tree's roots are unable to get water from the frozen ground. The tree sheds its leaves in the fall and becomes **dormant**, or inactive, for the winter. Having no leaves prevents the tree from losing moisture in cold, dry weather.

Why trees are important

Trees do many important jobs. They provide shelter and food for animals and release oxygen and water into the air. Trees also help save electricity. Buildings that are in the shade of trees need less air conditioning than those which are in direct sunlight.

*Roots help stop **erosion** by holding soil in place and soak up rainwater to prevent floods.*

*1. As the weather turns cold, a layer of **cork** develops at the end of each leaf's stalk.*

cork

chlorophyll

2. The chlorophyll in the leaf, which gives it its green color, starts to break down. As the chlorophyll disappears, the red, yellow, or orange color of the leaf begins to show through.

3. When the leaf has no chlorophyll left, its true color is the color we see.

4. Finally, the leaf dies and falls to the ground.

Plants and people

Plants help us in many ways. We use plants to make foods such as flour, peanut butter, and sugar. Cotton, linen, and rayon are fabrics we can make by weaving together plant fibers. Other products people get from plants include medicines, lumber, rubber, and paper.

Medicines that are used to treat cancer, heart disease, and infections are all made from plants. Products such as toothpaste and mouthwash also have ingredients made from plants.

Fruits and vegetables

We get fruits and vegetables directly from plants. Fruit is the part of the plant that contains new seeds. Tomatoes are fruit. The other parts of plants that we eat are called vegetables. Carrots are roots, broccoli is a group of many flowers, and peas are seeds.

People and animals eat many kinds of fruit. Oranges are a good source of vitamin C.

(above) Trees are used to make paper such as facial tissues, cardboard, and newsprint. The paper is put on large rolls. By recycling paper we can help save trees.

(right) The clothing worn by these boys is made of fibers from cotton plants. The rope is made of other plant fibers. The tire is made partly from the sap of rubber trees.

People love the beauty of plants and trees. Going on a hike surrounded by plants makes you feel great!

Threats to plants

Plants are being harmed in all their habitats. Forests, grasslands, wetlands, and oceans are being destroyed. When plants are destroyed, the animals that depend on them also suffer.

Oceans

People drill the ocean floor for oil. Leaks or spills from offshore oil rigs and the tankers that carry the oil to other places kill many living things, including the plants on which animals feed.

Oceans and seas make up the largest habitat on Earth and are home to the biggest and smallest animals. Oceans contain tiny plantlike organisms that can make their own food. They provide food for millions of sea creatures. Chemicals from factories and sewage from cities harm living things. Oil **tankers**, or ships, can spill oil into the ocean killing both plants and animals.

Wetlands

Millions of plants and animals make their home in wetlands. Pollution and pesticides poison wetland areas, and people drain wetlands to grow crops or build houses. When wetlands are drained, water plants die. Migrating birds that use wetlands as resting grounds lose their source of food.

Forests

Half of the species of plants and animals on Earth are found in forests. Rain forests are home to many kinds of plants from which medicines are made. People cut down trees to make wood and paper products and to clear space for farming. Many tropical rain forests are being burned to make room for cattle ranches.

Trees and plants store carbon in their trunks or stems. When forests burn, carbon dioxide is released into the air, causing air pollution. Air pollution is harmful to people and animals

Exploring plants

How many plants can you name? Take a nature walk and write down the names of all the plants you see. Draw pictures of plants you cannot name and look them up in a plant book. Do the activities on these pages to find out more about plants.

Grow a carrot top

The carrot is a vegetable that stores energy in its root. Cut off the leafy top and the bottom three-quarters of a fresh carrot. Stick toothpicks in the carrot and place it over a glass of water so the bottom of the carrot touches the water. Using the energy the carrot has stored in its root, the top of the carrot will grow tall and leafy again.

Plants and light

What happens if a plant does not get enough light? Using paper clips, attach a piece of paper to a leaf to block sunlight from getting through. Put the plant in a sunny spot. After a few days, take off the paper. How does the covered part of the leaf look?

Plants and carbon dioxide

What happens when a plant does not get enough air? Cover the leaves of a plant with petroleum jelly. The sunlight will be able to reach the leaf, but air will not be able to get through. Observe how the leaf looks after a few days and nights without air.

Be a tree doctor

Examine the trees and plants in a park close to your home or schoolyard. Look at the the leaves, flowers, branches, and trunks of trees. What types of animals make their homes in the trees? Are there signs of damage to the trees caused by storms, insects, animals, or people? Write a report on your findings.

A work of art

Choose a plant or tree to sketch. Sketch the whole plant or just a part such as a flower or a cone. Draw as many details as you can on your plant picture.

How old am I?

Count the rings on this trunk to find out!

Build your own terrarium

A **terrarium** is a container in which plants are kept and observed. Use a fish tank or a large jar to make a terrarium. First, put a layer of potting soil in the bottom. Next, plant several kinds of plants in the soil, and place rocks and sticks beside them. Choose small plants, such as mosses and ferns, which will grow slowly. To keep the leaves moist, spray the plants with water every day.

Words to know

active trapper Describing a carnivorous plant that uses movement to trap its prey

alga A tiny organism that can make its own food. Several alga are called algae.

bulb A tightly packed bundle of leaves that store food for the plant

carnivorous Describing something that eats meat

chlorophyll A green pigment found in plants that allows them to make food

conifer A tree that keeps its leaves all year; an evergreen

erosion The process by which materials, such as rock or soil, are worn away

fungus A kingdom whose species, such as mold and mushrooms, get their food from both living and dead things. Several fungus are called fungi.

germinate To grow from a seed into a plant

greenhouse effect Describing how gases such as carbon dioxide keep heat trapped within the Earth's atmosphere

host A plant or animal that supports a parasite

photosynthesis The process by which plants use the sun's energy to turn water and carbon dioxide into glucose and release oxygen as a byproduct

pigment A natural material that gives a plant or animal its color

prothallium A small, delicate plant that grows from a spore and can produce another plant such as a fern. More than one are called prothallia

rhizome An underground stem

root The underground part of a plant, which anchors it and absorbs water and nutrients

seed A capsule made by most plants, from which a new plant grows

shrub A plant with a woody trunk that has branches close to the ground

spore A tiny cell made by mosses and ferns that can grow into a new plant

stem The part of a plant that holds it upright, connecting the roots to leaves and flowers

tuber A thick, underground stem from which new plants grow

Index

1 2 3 4 5 6 7 8 9 0 Printed in the U.S.A. 9 8 7 6 5 4 3 2 1 0